# Tips for Trading

A Complete Guide to Avoid Mistakes and Always Do the Right Move

Steven Moore

Table of Contents

# Common Mistakes When You Start Trading

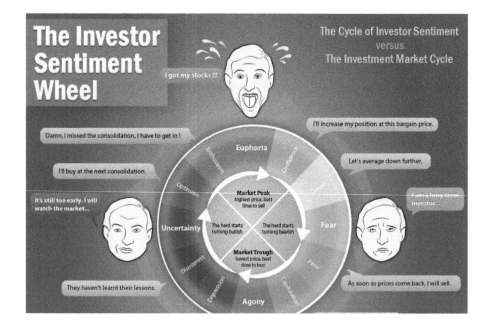

Options are one of the greatest wealth-building tools and a quick way to lose all your trading capital. Options can fall to zero or go up 1000%, and you must have a plan for either possibility. By deploying small amounts of capital and capturing full moves in your favor, they can a good asymmetric risk management tool and keep you from over-leveraging your account.

Here are the biggest and most common pitfalls that new options traders encounter.

New options traders buy far out-of-the-money options without understanding how the odds are stacked against them. Suppose the Delta is only .10 on your option. In that case, you have less than a 1 in 10 chance of your option expiring in the money. Even if you get a move in your favor, your far out of the money option won't increase in value until the Delta expands enough to overcome the time decay.

It takes a large move in price to increase the value of out-of-the-money options. The odds of it expiring in the money must increase enough to drive up the contract price. New options traders often become frustrated when the price moves in their favor and their out-of-the-money option goes down in value. In most instances, this is gambling and not trading. Always try to be the casino and not the gambler.

It's not wise to trade illiquid options because you can lose 10% or more of your capital at risk entering and exiting your trade if the volume doesn't tighten the spread. Research to see how much it will cost you to get in and out of the trade before you get started. Option spreads of .10 to .50 are preferable. A .10 bid/ask spread on an option will cost you $10 to get into the trade and then $10 to get out. A 100 share contract times .10 cents a share equals $10 each way. This is a $20 round trip, in addition to your commission fee, and this only covers one contract. A $1 bid/ask spread will cost you $100 in slippage to get in and then $100 or more to get out of one contract. This is an operating expense that adds up over time. The moment you enter a one-contract option with a $1 bid/ask spread, you are already down $100 in slippage. I only trade in the most liquid options contracts

I can find and stay away from the low-volume markets that will slowly eat away at my trading capital.

Look for options that are in line with your trading time frame. Give your trade enough time to work. If you plan on Apple going to $110 in 2 months, then don't buy a weekly $110 strike call because it will run out of time and expire worthless. Instead, buy a two-month out-call option that won't expire before your trade has time to work. You must be right about the price *and* period; just one or the other is not good enough to be profitable.

One of the most important things to remember is that the implied volatility is priced into options above the normal time value before earnings announcements or an uncertain event. The Vega premium disappears after the event comes and goes. For example, if an at-the-money weekly Apple call option and put option is trading at $10 above normal time value on the day of an earnings announcement, the day after that, $10 in Vega value will be gone. The trade is only profitable if the option's intrinsic value going in the money of the strike price is more than enough to replace the lost Vega value.

When trading through a volatile event like earnings, you must be right about the price's magnitude; the direction alone is not enough. Buying options through earnings has a low probability of success because the option sellers give themselves many Vega values to cover their risk. Because of this, it's very difficult to overcome the Vega collapse. Many will opine about the few times the move was not priced in, but that is an uncommon event.

There are two ways to use options to capture a simple price move. Options traders must understand that to make money out of the money options, they must be right about the price, the time to get to the price, the magnitude of the price move, and if the price rises enough to overcome Theta's cost and Vega above the strike price. However, with the money options, you take on the risk of intrinsic value and only need to be right about the direction. The money options have littlv Theta or Vega value. They are almost all intrinsic value and have high Deltas of over .90. With the right liquidity and going deep enough, the money options can be used like synthetic stocks with less risk.

Don't risk more than you would when trading stocks. I never advise against risking more than 1% of trading capital on any one trade, and the same applies to options. If you can only trade 100 shares of Apple, then only trade one Apple in the money option contract. If your trading capital is large enough to handle trading 1000 shares of Twitter in your normal stock trading account, then trade ten contracts of Twitter options. Don't trade too large with options. They can double and triple in price, but they can also go to zero. Options can move so fast that they are difficult to implement effective stop losses. It's much easier to have option trades be all, or nothing trades with very small positions. With weekly options, a 50% stop loss on an option is the best you will be able to manage. Stop losses must be on the stock chart where they have value and not at a random option price decline level. That's why I prefer all-or-nothing option trades.

Unlike stocks that are owned in a company, options are derivatives of stocks and are contracts that will expire.

They are not assets, and they are bets. Options are a zero-sum game; there is a winner for every loser. To be on the winning side, you need to trade with the odds in your favor. If you are a premium seller, sell the deep out of the money options with little chance of worth anything. Option buyers can buy to open the money options in the direction of the current markvt trend. Option premium sellers can sell to open put options under the hottest stocks' support during bull markets and sell calls on the stocks in downtrends.

Avoid the temptation of selling puts on junk stocks and calls on monster stocks in strong trends because this can be dangerous. Don't buy low probability far out of the money lottery tickets, and then sell. Don't cap your upside on a hot stock by selling a covered call, instead buy a call option and get the upside for a small investment of capital. Be on the right side of the probabilities, manage your risk, and you will do very well over the long-term.

# Risks That You Need to Avoid

| | Rating | Technical Risks | For Cost / Schedule Risks |
|---|---|---|---|
| **Likelihood** | 1 | < 0.5% | < 20% |
| | 2 | 0.5% to 1% | 21% to 40% |
| | 3 | 1% to 5% | 41% to 60% |
| | 4 | 5% to 10% | 61% to 80% |
| | 5 | >10% | > 80% |

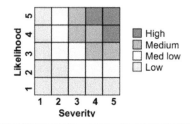

| Severity | | | | | |
|---|---|---|---|---|---|
| Rating | 1 | 2 | 3 | 4 | 5 |
| **Technical** | Minor inconvenience; < 5% utility loss, e.g., infrequent safehold transition without damage | Significant impairment of margin or secondary missions; 6-15% utility loss, e.g. degradation in thermal control, ACS, or battery | Major impairment of margin, design life, or secondary missions; 16-45% utility loss, e.g. frequent safeholding or power shedding, high noise | Severe impact; 46-75% loss of utility, e.g. permanent loss of redundancy, failure to meet key mission objective, early mission termination | Catastrophic Beginning of Life (BOL) failure |
| **Schedule** | Minimal or no impact | Erode segment schedule margin by > 5% | Erode system schedule margin by > 5% or segment margin by > 25% | Erode system schedule margin by > 25% | Delay key effectivity date or event, e.g. delay of launch, delivery of missile warning capability |
| **Cost** | < $200K | $200K to $1M | $1M to $10M | $10M to $50M | > $50M |

(Left column label: Magnitude of Impact)

## Understanding Options Risks

The options trading process does carry some risks with it. Understanding these risks and taking mitigating steps will make you not just a better trader but a more profitable one as well. Many traders love options trading because of the immense leverage that this kind of trading affords them. Should an investment work out as desired, then the profits are often quite high. You can expect returns of between 10%, 15%, or even 20% with stocks. However, when it comes to options, profit margins over 1,000% are possible.

These kinds of trades are possible due to nature and leverage offered by options. A savvy trader realizes that they can control an almost equivalent number of shares as a traditional stock investor but at a fraction of the cost. Therefore, when you invest in options, you can spend a tiny amount of money to control a large number of shares. This kind of leverage limits your risks and exposure compared to a stock investor.

As an investor or trader, you should never spend more than 3% to 5% of your funds in any single trade. For instance, if you have $10,000 to invest, you should not spend more than $300 to $500 on any trade.

Also, as a trader, you are not just mitigating against potential risks but are also looking to take advantage of the leverage. This is also known as gaining a professional trader's edge. While it is crucial to reduce the risk through careful analysis and selection of trades, you should also aim to make huge profits and enjoy big returns on your trades. There will always be some losses, and as a trader, you should get to appreciate this. However, your major goal as a trader should be to ensure that your wins are much larger than any losses you may suffer.

All types of investment opportunities carry a certain level of risk. However, options trading carries a much higher risk of loss. Therefore, ensure that you have a thorough understanding of the risks and always be on the lookout. Also, these kinds of trades are possible due to nature and leverage offered by options. A savvy trader realizes that they can control an almost equivalent number of shares as a traditional stock investor but at a fraction of the cost.

Therefore, when you invest in options, you can spend a tiny amount of money to control a large number of shares. This kind of leverage limits your risks and exposure compared to a stock investor.

## Time Is Not on Your Side

You need to keep in mind that all options have an expiration date and expire in time. When you invest in stocks, time is on your side most of the time. However, things are different when it comes to options. The closer an option gets to its expiration, the quicker it loses its value and earning potential.

Options deterioration is usually rather rapid, and it accelerates in the last days until expiration. As an investor, ensure that you only invest dollar amounts that you can afford to lose. The good news, though, is that there are a couple of actions that you can take to get things on your side.

- Trade mostly in options with expiration dates that are within the investment opportunity

- Buy options at or very near the money

- Sell options any time you think volatility is highly-priced

- Buy options when you believe that volatility is underpriced

**Prices Can Move Pretty Fast**

Options are highly leveraged financial instruments. Because of this, prices tend to move pretty fast. Options prices can move huge amounts within minutes and sometimes even seconds. This is unlike other stock market instruments like stocks that move-in hours and days.

Small movements in the price of a stock can have huge implications on the underlying stock's value. You need to be vigilant and monitor price movements often. However, you can generate profits without monitoring activity on the markets twenty-four hours a day.

As an investor or trader, you should seek opportunities were earning a significant profit is immense. The opportunity should be sufficiently robust so that pricing by seconds will be of little concern. In short, search for opportunities that will lead to large profits even when you are not accurate when selling.

When structuring your options, you should ensure that you use the correct strike prices and expiration months to cut most of the risk. You should also consider closing out your trades well before the expiration of options. This way, time value will not dramatically deteriorate.

## Naked Short Positions Can Result in Substantial Losses

Anytime that your naked short option presents a high likelihood of substantial and sometimes even unlimited losses. Shorting put naked means selling stock options with no hedging of your position.

When selling a naked short, it simply implies that you are actually selling a call option or even a put option but without securing it using an option position, stock or cash. It is advisable to sell a put or a call in combination with other options or with stocks. Remember that whenever you short sell a stock, you are, in essence, selling borrowed stock. Sooner or later, you will have to return the stock.

Fortunately, with options, there is no borrowing of stock or any other security.

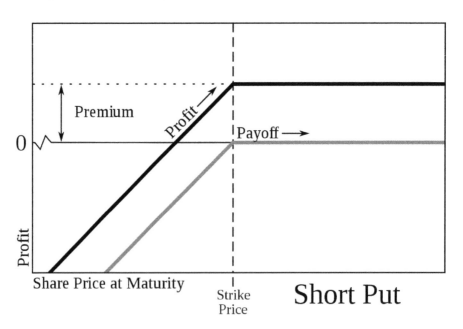

## Swing Trading Stocks

You can make utilize a few strategies when swing-trading stocks. I have introduced a swing trade case dependent on Fibonacci retracement signs (this is discussed presently). You will see that the letters A, B, C, and D. speak to significant pieces of the outline. Three of them are the most significant in any trade: the passage point(A), the left point (C) and the stop misfortune (C). These focuses must be remembered for any swing trading framework. While the passage point is fixed, the stop misfortune point and the left level don't need to be fixed. Contingent upon the trading system utilized, they can be moved in time with value activity and afterward activated just when a specific specialized set-up happens. In the model over, the assessed time allotment for the trade is around seven days. This is significant for each trade – to know the run-of-the-mill time over which your swing trade will unfurl. It assists with having the option to amplify the capability of the trade and helps compelling observing.

## Five swing trading strategies for stocks

I have assembled five swing trade procedures to help you spot openings and direct your trade from the passage point to the left point. Study them completely, then apply them to loads of your decision to discover section and leave focuses.

## 1 – Fibonacci retracement

The Fibonacci retracement design is a lot of proportions utilized principally to perceive backing and opposition levels on stock graphs. It depends on the perception that stock costs will, in general, alter course at specific rates while on a pattern before they proceed toward that pattern. This retracement is the thing that the swing dealer searches for as the passage point. Fibonacci proportions – 23.6%, 38.2% and 61.8% depend on common scientific counts. Plotting even lines at these levels can assist with foreseeing retracement points on a pattern.

The Fibonacci design doesn't have a half level; however, numerous merchants likewise utilize this level since it has been seen that costs invert, having gone most of the way in a pattern bearing retracement.

This is the thing that you need to pay special mind to when utilizing the Fibonacci design. When a down pattern remembers 61.8%, you need to enter a transient sell position. All the more along these lines, when this level is filling in as an obstruction point on this pattern. Your leave point ought to be around the 23.6% Fibonacci level. Once more, this level ought to fill in as a help level on this pattern.

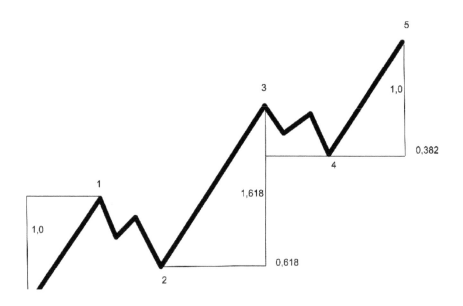

## 2 – Support and obstruction triggers

Specialized Analysis (TA) is basically about distinguishing backing and opposition levels with the end goal of anticipating future examples. Utilizing value activity specialized investigation alone, you can shape a triumphant technique.

A help level in basic terms is that value level where the cost gets to dropping goes up once more. What happens is that at this value area, there is more prominent purchasing pressure (for the most part since individuals think the stock is as of now oversold) than the selling pressure. This powers the stock cost back up. Along these lines, you are hoping to submit a purchase request when the cost gets to this level and spot your 'stop-misfortune's simply beneath the helpline if there should arise an occurrence of a breakout. Numerous elements can control the exit of this position. A decent practice is to exit almost a perceived obstruction level.

The obstruction line is only the direct inverse of the help. It is the value extend at which the ascent in the cost of a stock is stopped to such an extent that it starts to plunge. By and by, now, selling pressure has defeated the purchasing pressure. The swing dealer along these lines hopes to enter a short position when the value contacts the obstruction level and leaves this situation close to a perceived help point. The 'stop-loss' of this trade should be put over the opposition point to represent a breakout.

A significant thing to think about backings and opposition levels is that when a pattern changes (from an upward pattern to the descending or the other way around), the levels likewise change jobs. The help presently shapes a solid obstruction level, and the opposition levels structure solid help levels for the new pattern.

## 3 – Channel trading

This methodology works for stocks that are indicating extremely solid patterns and are additionally in a channel. The pattern development shapes a channel, with the upper band being the most noteworthy stock cost during the period and the lower band, the least stock cost during this period. The section focuses on channel trading is natural. You need to get in a short position when the value hits the upper band of the channel. What's more, you need to get into a long position when it hits the lower band. Leave focuses and stop misfortune levels ought to be talked about in technique 2. A significant thing to note when channel trading a pattern is that you trade with the pattern. How about we make this understood. If the pattern is upward, just enter long places (that is, the point at which the costs hit the lower band). If the pattern is downwards, just search for sell section focuses. The main exclusion to this circumstance is if there is a breakout and you can affirm a pattern inversion is fast approaching.

## 4 – 10-and 20-day SMA

SMA represents Simple Moving Averages. These are devices that help cover out value information up a timeframe. They are determined utilizing straightforward math. The normal of costs over a specific period is taken and connected to the normal of the following time frame's cost to make a smooth bend. The smoothness of the bend relies upon the time of the SMA. For example, a 10-day SMA includes the end costs throughout the previous ten days of stock and partitions it by 10 to get normal. It does this ordinarily to get another normal. A little period moving normally will give more unpleasant bends than an extensive stretch one since they respond all the more rapidly to value changes. By and large, the moving midpoints help to take out the "clamor" of the costs. They can be utilized on outlines of whenever outline (1 moment, 5minute, week by week or month to month). SMA is what you can call slacking markers. This implies they give you chronicled information and just refreshed at the end of the period.

This system utilizes two SMA – the 10-day and 20-day time frame SMA. You put the two on the graph. You watch for a traverse the other. When the SMA – 10 crosses over the SMA – 20, this is a sign to go long because it proposes that an upswing will start. When the SMA – 10 goes underneath the SMA – 20, a shot sign is demonstrated. One can anticipate a bearish pattern. For transparency, it is prompted that you utilize various hues for the two lines. Many outlining programming gives this.

### 5 – MACD Crossover

The MACD is another device that is extremely well known among swing dealers. It is a blend of two moving midpoints. One fills in as the MACD line, while the other is the signature line. The signs for passage are produced likewise as the system above. When the MACD line goes over the signature line, it demonstrates an upward pattern; thus, a long position is flagged. A sell trade is recommended when the MACD line goes underneath the signature line. This implies a bearish pattern is impending. As an s stock swing merchant, you at that point search for the second intersection of these lines as the sign for an exit because a pattern inversion is proposed.

There is a zero line in the MACD. The MACD line wavered around it. This development likewise produces trade signals. Buy trading signals are produced when the 'MACD crosses' over the zero lines and sell signals on the off chance that it crosses beneath it.

## Swing Trading Options

An alternative is a money-related subordinate. It is a real agreement that gives the purchaser the option to purchase or sell a security at a specific date (the activity date). The merchant furthermore holds a promise to fulfill the trade, which is to purchase or sell, if the purchaser rehearses the choice before its end. The purchasing and selling of investment opportunities are controlled by the US Securities and trade commission.

Numerous procedures are utilized by the individuals who trade alternatives. Every one of them anyway includes either purchasing or selling at least one choice. They do this in heading or unbiased reaction to showcase see on the underlying resource.

They ordinarily utilize uncommonly arranged diagrams called alternative 'payout or result profiles' to get a pictorial perspective on what the procedure will yield more gains on its 'running-out date for an assortment of unique sell esteems, for example, the one demonstrated as follows.

From the diagram over, the blue line shows the way wherein the trade will

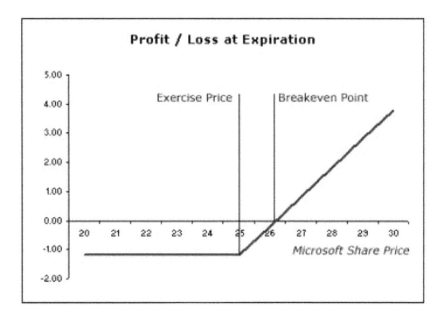

Come into benefit if the market goes past the make back the initial investment point. In any case, the chart doesn't show that a merchant can take benefit by shutting the trade before its lapse. This is conceivable when you can sell the choice for more than you got it. This is commonly the target when swinging trading choices.

In case you're not effectively acquainted with Options trading, presently would be a decent time to do some examination.

The swing trading Options technique has three primary advantages:

- Profit age

- Limited hazard presentation

- You can trade significant expense stocks with an extremely little record.

The general techniques with regards to alternatives trading are the call and put choices. The call choice initiates the acquisition of stocks while the put alternatives show an interest in selling a stock.

It is moderately simple to figure out how to swing trade alternatives since it is a directional technique for the market. The stunts underneath will give you a thought of a straightforward technique for swing trading choices. When you become familiar with this, you can adjust it as you advance your aptitudes. Swing trading alternatives aren't entangled. It offers a course to more make sure about benefits than most systems.

Here are six stages of comprehending swing trading for Options in their most basic components

### Step 1: How to Select the Right Stocks

Regardless of how ingenious your system is, you would wind up blowing through your record on the off chance you are trading inappropriate stocks. Choosing the correct stock can be overwhelming when you don't have the foggiest idea of what you are searching for, seeing as there are handfuls recorded on the major exchange markets. A basic method is to have a part watchlist that you work with the main stocks on the planet.

At that point, you watch this rundown for enormous moves to pick the correct contender for your system. The way to choose those with the biggest moves is you need to exploit the value swings. You can go above and beyond to check the reason for this huge rate of development in cost. If it is brought about by essential variables, it improves the stock of a competitor.

## Step 2: How to Assess the Market

Each market will be in a specific state when you enter. You should guarantee to check the history and, if conceivable, use devices (like the Bollinger groups) to survey the market to discover what state it is in. The market can either be in a pattern (upturn or downtrend) or not (going sideways). If the market is in a pattern, you need to figure out which pattern and the pattern's quality. For an upward pattern, you are searching for 'higher highs' and 'higher lows.' For a descending pattern, you are looking for lower lows and lower highs. You should remember that you should consistently go with the pattern. When there is an upturn, pick just call choices. When in a downtrend, pick just put choices.

A significant evaluation you should make next is the unpredictability in the market. It is ideal to go to little periods (5 mins, 10 mins, 60 minutes) to check this.

Realizing the unpredictability will assist you with settling on the lapse of your trade.

## Step 3: Decide your entry

This is perhaps the most significant choice to make because a couple of pips could have a significant effect. This is the place acceptable information on specialized and essential investigation comes to play. These are shrouded later right now. For the most part, the section cost is when you are wagering. The cost will go over or underneath at the termination time.

## Step 4: How to Select an Expiration time

A specialized investigation is the particular most significant decider of the decision of the lapse to pick. The decision of termination relies exclusively upon the time that specialized investigation was made. For the most part, while doing a specialized examination, brokers regularly utilize diverse periods to get by and large and explicit thought of the market development. Be that as it may, when deciding on a trade, there is the base time allotment at which point the significant investigation is completed. You need to utilize products of this time allotment while picking a termination. For example, if the TA is done on a brief diagram, your time-lapse should be 15 minutes, 30 minutes, 45 minutes, 60minutes... in a specific order. This makes your expectations simpler.

By and large, numerous dealers offer the best yields on the most limited terminations (30 secs, one moment). In any case, these courses of events forecast the most elevated hazard levels. The more extended the expiration, the lesser the hazard and the lesser the prize. I will encourage you to favor the month-to-month time allotment since this will take into account not so much risk but more precise TA.

## Step 5: Manage the trade

If you happen to enter the market during times of low instability, what you ought to do is to sell your choice before its terminations. Alternatives experience what is known as time rot. This essentially the decrease in the estimation of choice as the approaches its lapse. For example, an alternative worth $30 at its buy for 10 minutes when out of the cash may drop to about $ 29.50 in the initial 2 minutes and drop similarly as

$2 in the eighth moment. If it is in cash, the rate gain drops additionally as it arrives at its lapse should you decide to sell it. It can drop from an underlying 85% to 60%. It is shrewd to sell immediately when out of the cash or cash if you don't confide later on for the alternatives.

Swing trading alternatives can be a ground-breaking technique when aced. This needs a ton of practice and perseverance. Numerous alternatives dealers will, in general, need to make easy money. Along these lines, they trade exceptionally little league outlines. Swing merchants don't.

## Swing Trading Crypto

One of the methodologies that I will disclose to you is trading digital currency. For what reason do we put for the most part in crypto and blockchain-related resources? Since we accept they are one of the greatest insurgencies, this is the ideal time to get required before the market detonates to the upside and costs ascend at significant stocks level.

Another explanation that I like cryptographic forms of money and their market is that they are very unstable and give the regular person the likelihood to bring in genuine cash without contributing a great deal. It's anything but a mystery, truth be told, that each time the market begins to rise, individuals race into the quest for the "following enormous win," and the inquiry that circles is consistently the equivalent: "What will the following digital currency be that will go to 'the moon'?"

The issue with digital forms of money is that being a market that isn't yet directed in a few nations, the danger of siphons and dumps, control and extortion are practically around the bend. This is the reason I needed to cover them right now. Since they give an incredible chance, I am stressed that many individuals may get included without realizing what they are doing and will lose a ton of cash down the line. Here I need to give you what I do before putting resources into a specific resource and keeping it an economic wellspring of easy revenue.

Try not to begin until you read beneath for our rundown of helpful devices. These are essential for the examination of digital forms of money:

- Coincheckup.com - one of my preferred locales, offers substantially more information than other digital money checking destinations;

- Coinmarketcap.com - one of the most seasoned crypto value following locales, unmistakably more well-known than Coincheckup, yet offers less information;

- Blockfolio - another well-known digital money tracker. Presently we should get to the great stuff.

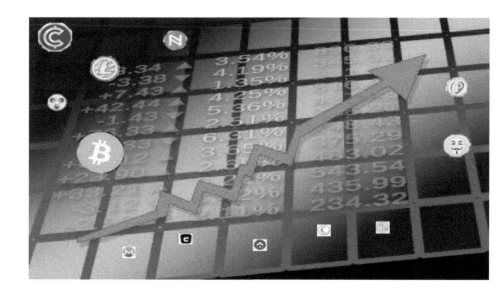

## Step 1 - Understanding your risk profile

Numerous individuals will encourage you to purchase "low capitalization."

Cryptographic forms of money and tokens (for example, somewhere in the range of 10 and 100 million dollars) have a more noteworthy open door for development as far as rate.

Even though this announcement is moderately right, you need to remember that the littler a coin is, the less secure it is to put resources into it. Why? Since the venture has a lot higher danger of falling flat.

In customary ventures, the vast majority point and are glad to get a yearly return of 3% - 4%; however they could be in genuine budgetary trouble if the contributed capital is lost, more often than not, progressively notable secure increasingly stable titles are chosen.

Others would rather be fulfilled distinctly with a yearly yield of 7% - 12%. These individuals could likewise be eager to lose all their speculation if things turn out badly. They would highlight a higher hazard given the financial mentality they have at the base for their situation.

These two unique gatherings of individuals have distinctive "chance profiles."

It is significant that in any buy you make in your life (in any event, for something "solid" like a vehicle), you do so intentionally about the budgetary hazard profile you can bear to take.

My sincere belief is that since something has higher odds of execution doesn't mean it is the best decision. Specifically, I have put primarily in the main five coins regarding capitalization since they are the most secure spot at this moment. Be that as it may, I generally assign a little piece of my portfolio, 10% to be exact, to low-top coins. How would I locate the most encouraging one?

Here is what I do.

**Step 2 - Identification of new coins or tokens**
There are three principle ways I generally use to locate the "new" coins or tokens:

- Through the posts of the Bitcointalk.org discussion, all the more unequivocally in the segment "Declarations (Altcoins)";

- In the subreddit/r/digital currency;

- In the "Recently Added" areas of Coincheckup and "As of late Added."

These are extraordinary assets to find intriguing coins with incredible return potential over a shorter timeframe. As of now stated, I just put in a limit of 10% of my capital into these underestimated ventures.

With each venture comes the likelihood to get defrauded, and in the crypto world, it happens more frequently than I might want to see. During the most recent three years of experience, I have built up a progression of rules that I follow to abstain from being defrauded. Here is the thing that will cause me to choose NOT to put resources into a benefit.

## Step 3 - Exclusion of coins and useless tokens/scams

One of the underlying impacts I do when I take a gander at new undertakings is to expose them to exacting criteria to evacuate "lighten" ventures from the rundown. Specifically:

- I don't purchase cryptographic forms of money from enterprises and divisions that I don't comprehend;

- I don't purchase cryptographic forms of money whose groups are inert in internet-based life correspondence;

- I don't purchase digital currencies whose new companies/affiliations/organizations are enrolled in nations where I can't approve a strong corporate substance;

- I don't purchase digital currencies on the off chance that I can't discover the colleagues (with specific thoughtfulness regarding the author) on LinkedIn and approve that they are genuine profiles;

- I don't purchase digital currencies whose groups receive spamming techniques and do forceful and non-enlightening promoting efforts on social and non-social channels;

- If a group is building a fresh out of the box innovation, I don't purchase the cryptographic money/token except if there is a definite specialized report clarifying how it functions;

- If digital money has a pre-ICO with a rebate, I tend not to get it. On the off chance that I did, it would just be for the situation where the markdown contrasted with the open ICO is negligible and the sum bought is "bolted" for a critical timeframe (to maintain a strategic distance from monstrous dumps after the open ICO);

- I don't purchase digital forms of money on the off chance that I don't utilize them actually as an end client.

To assist me with the procedure, I likewise utilize a progression of inquiries that permit me to get more inside and out and understand the genuine major estimation of a benefit. Specifically, I truly prefer to ask myself the accompanying inquiries:

- Would I utilize this digital currency as an end client?

- Would I follow through on that cost as a client?

- Does this task require the improvement of another innovation?

- What is the group's involvement with this decided course? Have they previously dealt with an effective organization? What was the presentation of this organization?

- Does the group have the capacity to build up this innovation? Our specialists and engineers perceived right now? =

- Is it clear how the venture will produce clients/clients?

- Why would they say they are utilizing the blockchain? Do they truly require it, or do they utilize the expression "blockchain" to publicity their task up? (Remember that as of now, much of the time, blockchain-based frameworks are moderate and costly).

Focus on absolutist proclamations. Each undertaking has negative perspectives and results; a genuine venture will help portray them, particularly the last mentioned.

On the off chance that I can see that each question has a positive answer, I will distribute a piece of my portfolio. I generally contribute long haul, and I will remain in a coin for in any event one year. If, in any capacity whatsoever, I don't feel sufficiently certain to place cash into a venture for in any event 52 weeks, then that implies that it is most likely better to take a gander at another.

Anticipating the following money that will make the blast is unimaginable, out there one can run over such a significant number of ventures dependent on nothing that despite everything underwrite many billions of dollars; similarly, òmany genuine tasks merit more, yet that neglects to stick out and gain perceivability contrasted with others. The brilliant principle is what applies in each budgetary market: differentiate. By expanding between a few coins, you diminish the hazard.

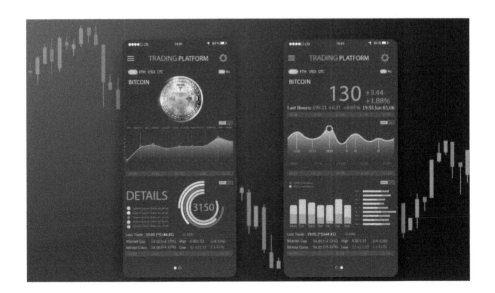

## Technical and Fundamental Analysis

Technical Analysis is the investigation of charts. Taking a gander at the graphs, the investigator can comprehend if that stock (or market) will rise or fall in the short, medium and long haul. The Fundamental Analysis rather puts together its figures regarding the "principal factors," like news, advertising gossipy tidbits, organization acquisitions, financial emergencies, political occasions, wars, and so on.

### Which is better between

Specialized Analysis and Fundamental Analysis? Who has never posed this inquiry? The appropriate response is basic; as consistently in speculations, there is no better alternative. It relies upon the financial specialist, on his method for working in the business sectors, on his hazard level, and so forth. There are the individuals who are in an ideal situation with one, and there are the individuals who are in an ideal situation with the other.

I, for one, love the Technical Analysis considerably more for certain reasons. Let me present some of them:

- Timing: Technical Analysis offers preferred Timing over Fundamental Analysis. Timing is "the ideal time to get into a position," the perfect time to enter the market. As I would see it, one of the principal ideas to prevail in the stock trade. If you utilize the correct planning, you can bear the cost of an extremely tight Stop Loss, so you can just lose a bit. So cut the misfortunes and let the rewards run, the brilliant standard of the stock trade. Timing is given by the key levels that are gotten without issues with the diagrams' investigation and afterward through Technical Analysis.

- Flexibility: Technical Analysis is more adaptable than Fundamental Analysis since it gives us key levels (for Stop Loss and Goals) in whenever outline.

- Discount: Technical Analysis limits the Fundamental Analysis, essential hypothesize of Technical Analysis. The diagram now incorporates all the components, all the news, all the wars, all the financial conditions, and so forth. Accordingly, if the cost has risen, the essentials will be bullish. If the cost has dropped, the basics will be bearish. I can just deal with the diagram in this manner.

Also, Fundamental Analysis has the deformity that specific news is hard to track for a typical financial specialist. When this news shows up, it is futile because somebody more intelligent than us has just utilized it and purchased (or sold) before us.

We close with a kind of "metropolitan legend" of trading and across-the-board conviction (however off-base) that many, despite everything, have today. Numerous financial specialists accept that the Technical Analysis serves to make interests for the time being and that the Fundamental Analysis serves to make long haul speculations. This isn't accurate. Both can be utilized to work in the short, medium, and long haul.

Such a large number of speculators will keep on valuing one and numerous to appreciate the other. A smart thought, now and then, is to utilize both, subsequently joining one's benefits with the other's upsides. The utilization of this idea has been clarified concerning asylum monetary forms and high return financial forms in Forex.

## Can technical and fundamental analysis be used together?

Although a specialized and essential investigation is considered inverse posts, many market members have made a triumphant mix. For instance, some primary investigators utilize specialized examination instruments to distinguish the best occasions to enter the market.

By the by, numerous specialized investigators abuse the monetary basics to help specialized signs. For instance, if a skilled example in the diagram shows the chance of selling, we can allude to the critical information to affirm this example's affirmation.

A blend of specialized and crucial investigation isn't welcomed by the "radicals" of the two thinking ways. However, the advantage we can get from completely understanding the specialized and central examiner's attitude is irrefutable.

## How to Keep Growing Your Skills

When you have built up a gainful trading system that creates an easy revenue every month, you can't travel to Thailand and carry on with the PC way of life right now. As the tycoon Dan Lok stated, it doesn't mean it will keep going forever because it works. I truly need this to soak in as it is one of the most significant thoughts from the whole book.

When things are going as arranged, the time has come to significantly increase down on your exertion and genuinely subscribe to authority. Specifically, there are two things that I'd like you to do once the primary benefits begin to come.

## Form Alliance with other traders and start a business

It is valid, making companionships, cooperations, and associations are central for manageability. Having individuals working in your field of interest close to you can be valuable. You can trade thoughts, feelings, and appeals. Then again, on the off chance that somebody believes that this sort of cooperation can be found among family members and companions, he will end up colliding with a divider. Companions and family members, if not as of now in the division, will be an enormous snag. They will be the individuals who, at each mistake, will point their finger at you, not because they don't cherish you, but since the cerebrum rejects everything that it doesn't comprehend. This is the reason I generally propose to chip away at your budgetary objectives all alone and to share what you are doing after merely getting the primary indication of accomplishment. Recall that your attitude is powerless at the previous stages, and even the scarcest investigation can make it down.

**Find a mentor**
Achievement leaves strides: nearly anything you might want to do to improve another person has just finished your life. It doesn't make a difference whether you are beginning a business, starting your trading venture, having an upbeat marriage, shedding pounds, stopping smoking, running a long-distance race, or just sorting out an ideal lunch. There is positively somebody who did it well indeed and has left a few pieces of information.

At the point when you can exploit these valuable hints, you will find that life

Resembles a game where you should come to an obvious conclusion, and all the dabs have just been recognized and sorted out by others. Just follow their venture and utilize their framework.

# Different Trading Styles

Since we have invested some energy discussing forex trading and how to begin on it and did all the exploration, the time has come to chip away at managing the genuine transferring styles. If the cash is a decent one (which you ought to have the option to decide from the exploration that you did previously), the time has come to choose the methodology you will use to begin. Remember that you are going with a well-known stock on the off chance, the cost will be high to start with, and it tends to be challenging to begin.

Before we check out the techniques you can use with monetary standards trading, we have to recall anything but a smart thought to pursue a stock. Pursuing infers that you will raise your buying cost quickly, considering how you are tense to get the offers instead of someone else. This is an out and out awful thing to work with because your sentiments are going to start running, and you will consistently spend essentially more on the stock (and every so often, it will be a dreadful stock) than it is worth. Over the long haul, the buyers who sought after the capital will find that the estimation of the 'stocks' will slump, and the cost will go a comparable way, making it hard to sell them using any means, on any occasion, for a setback.

Keep in mind that it is fundamental to pick a framework that you have to work with, and a short time later remains with it. A large segment of the philosophies that are recorded underneath, similarly as a part of the others that you may find or get some answers concerning in your work, are going to help you with making a tolerable pace of gainfulness in case you make sense of how to use them fittingly and you don't change strategies once in a while.

This is normal among amateurs. They place several exchanges and find that they are not making the millions they longed for; at that point, they rapidly get another strategy. While it is entirely conceivable that the system might be flawed, what we are managing mind here isn't letting your feelings settle on the choice for you. A procedure needs time to be demonstrated, fortunate or unfortunate. During that time, you will put a couple of exchanges that will o awful. You have to see how the system functions by testing. On the off chance that you change procedures after 2 or 3 appalling exchanges, you won't gain proficiency with any of them and be unable to settle with anybody in the long run. Give it time.

Fortunately, when you pick a technique to work with within monetary forms, you can evade the issues with pursuing or a portion of the different problems that can come up when utilizing financial standards and making a buy. You can pick from numerous methodologies, so you don't need to feel that you will have the option to utilize one and not feel good about it. A portion of the trading techniques that you might need to consider when working with monetary forms include:

**Swing trading**
Regarding working with swing trading, the financial specialist will purchase and afterward likewise sell their security in only one day, once in a while doing it a few times during this day with at any rate one of their stocks. Fortunes can be made with this sort of exchange, yet they can likewise be immediately lost. To get swing trading to work, you have to have a great deal of understanding and information in your commercial center, a great methodology, and adequate capital. You can't get into it at last, and you should have the option to think unmistakably to hold your misfortunes under wraps.

Various advantages are going with swing trading, including:

1. The potential benefits that you can win will be immense because you get more than one exchange that is beneficial during the day.

2. The hazard that accompanies the stock or organization changing will be diminished because you are not clutching the stocks for that long. It isn't likely that the organization is going to change in only a day.

You will also find some disadvantages that accompany the swing trading choice, so individuals decide to use one of the different trading techniques. A portion of the cons that you will discover with swing trading include:

- You need to have a record balance that is enormous before you can even begin.

- Individuals who are not used to working in the financial exchange and can't control their feelings well can rapidly lose a great deal of cash.

- Since you have to utilize an edge account, this sort of trading can get you to lose more cash-flow than you put in, which can be extremely risky right now.

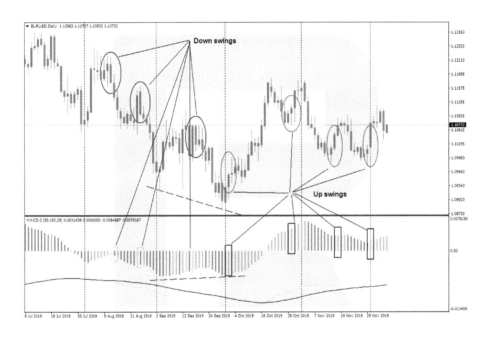

## Momentum Trading

The accompanying method that you may need to go with is energy trading. This is a framework that the money-related master would use if the stocks are moving quickly, similarly to a high volume, going in one course. Many financial specialists will play on an upward force concerning monetary standards because they are not typically accessible for a short deal.

Stocks that have power are because there is some buzz going on around the capital, for example, through the news or because of bits of gossip. To find these stocks, you ought to do some assessment and read through social affairs, message sheets, and the news to see what's going on. You should have the choice to find two or three stocks that are getting a great deal of thought without a moment's delay, which infers that specialists will play the stock hard to get the expense to go one way, and a short time later, they will take their advantage before everything goes diving again.

There should be some examination that goes into utilizing this choice. You have to set aside the effort to observe how trading on the stock is doing before making the buy. Those that can be finished with force have a genuinely high volume and shares moving either a lot higher or contrasted with the market. You will have the option to keep an eye out for these signs by taking a gander at graphs and watching the Level 2 provides and the cost estimate activity.

So after you have a once-over of the stocks that you should use, the opportunity has arrived to make the purchase. You should get it as quick as would be reasonable, at as low of an expense as you would find in random happenings before the vitality starts to go down again. When you claim the monetary forms, you should be all set, watching the market adjustments, taking a gander at graphs, and checking whether there are any new filings or news. When you spot any 'negative' surrounding the stock, for instance, dreadful news, horrendous markers, or a negative example, you should endeavor to do a smart idea to cut the young ladies before continuing ahead; this can't help industry where you suffer it to check whether it gives indications of progress.

On the other hand, if the vitality props up, you will need to grip the stocks and hold up until a part of the offers starts to aggregate. If the energy is going up when you get these offers and they are adequately high for you to

Consider, you may need to go with one of them.

The energy can stop going up whenever and could begin to lower, so take an offer you are OK with before the tides start to change. There might be an opportunity of procuring more if you clutch them longer, yet if you hang on excessively long, you will lose everything, so it is smarter to get what you can out of them.

A portion of the advantages that you will have the option to see with energy trading include:

- The monetary standards are frequently going to be the ones that move the most when energy begins to move, which implies that you can rake in boatloads of cash in a short measure of time.

- You will have the choice to find a tremendous amount of information through message sheets and various conversations to pick the stocks that are straightforwardly for you.

- While this is a phenomenal strategy for taking a significant salary in a tiny proportion of time, there are moreover a couple of cons that you should pay a unique mind to. A part of the disadvantages of using power trading include:

- Sometimes the monetary forms will be unstable, so your chance to sell and cause a benefit can be too short to even think about earning anything.

- Companies that have weakening motivation can once in a while slow down out a force run.

- Some individuals will utilize this thought to get more individuals to need their stocks. They will counterfeit the buzz and the news, so you should be cautious about working with them.

## Swing Trading

Another alternative that you can work with is swing trading. This kind of trading is acceptable if you take a shot at a stock that can move around in a brief timeframe period. This usually will be for stocks that will move inside the day; however, it can go for as long as four days. This sort will utilize a specialized investigation to search for a stock that may have energy at their cost over the present moment. With this one, you won't be that keen on the capital estimations, yet instead the patterns and examples of their cost.

In an ideal market, the shares are going to exchange beneath or over pattern

Esteem, or a moving normal. The monetary forms are going to utilize this as both the opposition and bolster levels. When you are toying around with the graphs, you will have the alternative to see many moving midpoints, which will fit the expense exercises, helping with trading decisions. Someone who has been in the money-related trade for a long time would understand that they should buy near the typical moving base, yet they would sell before it shows up at the target moving frequently.

Many stars can accompany this choice:

This is a good style for beginners trying to get into the market and still make some profits.

Home runs are not usually going to be done with swing trading, but if you catch the beginning of a new uptrend, there is the possibility of getting large profits.

You can utilize the fundamentals of this sort of trading in any market that you might want. Huge board stocks, futures, XCM, and Forex likewise use swing trading.

While many positives accompany monetary standards, there are also a couple of things you have to keep an eye out for. Swing trading can't choose that everybody will be partial to. A portion of the cons of picking swing trading as your technique include:

It is elusive that ideal market where specific cash will wind up trading between the obstruction and the help levels. This can get significantly harder to foresee when there is a solid downtrend or a solid upswing busy working.

Currencies can make it hard to time your buys the right way, especially when dealing with dilution on the stock you purchased.

**Technical Trading**
Technical trading is a good option to go for when you are looking at your trading strategy points. This one will use a Technical Analysis to help you find the right stocks that you would like to trade and help you set up your entry and then exit points to reduce losses if they would occur. Someone who decides to go with this kind of trading is

Going to use 'trading charts' to observe the whole record of the stock, take the time to observe indicators that are going on, and then identify the trends and patterns that are going on with the price.

Some indicators are available for use to work with technical trading. Some of these include:

- Strength indicators: these are the indicators that will compare the asset's current price to its historical prices. This comparison shows the strength of the stock. Most traders use the Relative Strength Index (RSI) for this comparison. You would find it on all charting platforms. It shows oversold and overbought levels for any stock. This can guide a trader to know what kind of trade to enter.

- Moving averages: they are popularly referred to as Mas. The moving average is an indicator generated by averaging out the price levels over so much time. These can help you see how regularly the stock developments are either beneath or over their midpoints. These are known as hybrids and can sometimes show breakdowns and breakouts also, something that is also imperative to a broker who is attempting to select what stock they might want to work with.

- Pattern examination: this is the assessment of your graphs to recognize value developments, for example, shapes that surface in history. Sometimes you can see wedges, triangles, cups, handles, and more for the stock you want to work with. These formations can sometimes be used to see into the future and determine if there will be any downward or upward movement. Market forces often cause them, but one showing up, whether it is natural or not, will affect that stock's action.

- 'Range analysis': this is where you will use a few different things together, such as the price range and the closing and opening prices, to figure out where your resistance and support levels are. With this, you will easily spot out the best purchase and sell points and tell you other information, such as the breakdown and breakout levels with the stock.

- Gap analysis: this one will be done when you can find gaps in the charts you are looking at. A gap is going to be a spot that is inside the chart, which a price will cause at the opening that is higher than what it was at the close of the previous period. The idea behind here is that these gaps are usually going to be filled, so you will be able to figure out the buy prices since you know that the price will go back down to fill up this gap before it goes higher.

These options will need you to use analysis to figure out when to enter the market, how long to hold on to the currencies and throw them away to get the most profit possible while limiting your losses. There are many benefits of using this kind of strategy, including:

Many people are on the forums and the boards, which will help you learn how to use 'Technical Analysis' and talk to you about identifying these hot stocks.

Inside of currencies, these technical moves can be pretty strong. This is because TA is to help you judge a stock and the way the price will move.

While numerous individuals will utilize this alternative to settle on their trading choices, you should note a couple of demerits. These are:

'Bashers and pumper's can make practically all diagrams seem as though they are negative or positive, with expectations of attracting financial specialists without experience into doing the activity that they need.

Without paying attention to some of the fundamentals, such as the news, a trade that looks good in this analysis could quickly turn around in just a few minutes, and you could lose out.

Technical analysis can be a bit complex and difficult for many traders.

**Scalping**
One of the different procedures that you can utilize when working in monetary forms is known as scalping. This is when the financial specialist will make a few exchanges to make

some little benefits on one of the stocks that truly doesn't move during that day. The hawker is going to utilize the offer and request that spread make this work. They will purchase their offers at the enormous or someplace near it; they would then pivot and make a little benefit. This one won't make them a huge amount of cash; however, it is better than nothing on the off chance that you plan it outright and the market isn't moving.

These techniques can help you build more profits quickly. While you may just make a couple of dollars on each exchange, when you do several of these, you can rake in so much cash every day. This is, in some cases, considered swing trading. Yet, know that all swing trading can't. This procedure will progress admirably some of the time, yet you should be cautious because most stocks won't remain steady, and you may wind up with one that goes down in an incentive as the day progressed.

There are a couple of advantages that originate from utilizing the scalping technique in your trading methodology. A portion of these advantages include:

For the most part, your currencies will have a large spread, giving you a good profit.

Currencies are sometimes going to trade sideways right after they finish with a big move or trying to break through the resistance level.

When you buy at the offer and afterward sell immediately at the ask, you will at present get the most reduced cost on your stock, and it diminishes the risk when you sell as fast as conceivable before things can change.

There are a couple of negatives that can come up from utilizing the scalping procedure for your trading. Some disadvantages of going with this strategy include:

Currencies can be hard to do this with as a result of their weak volume.

This process is going to make you neutralize your market creators, and this makes it troublesome.

Since monetary standards are a high hazard and this alternative is just going to give you a limited quantity of benefit, it may not be

The best. If you need to check it out, it isn't awful, yet a few people don't think the hazard merits the prize.

These methodologies have been utilized regarding working in monetary forms, and it is imperative to make sense of which technique you might want to use for your necessities. You can select any of them and see some achievement; however, you should be cautious. You won't see the great outcomes you need if you are skirting everywhere and not staying with a decent system. The individuals who are the best with monetary forms, just as with a portion of the other speculation choices, are the ones who will select one technique and stick with it. Consider a portion of the methodologies that we discussed right now. Pick the one that works the best with your requirements and help you make the greatest benefit in monetary standards.

Regardless of what system you use, there are best practices that all accomplished and effective brokers watch. These are the keys that will enable you to succeed. These things are not simply something that you read because their actual embodiment is doing, so make certain to apply them to all your exchanges. Here are the best trading rehearses that you should know:

## Make your discoveries

Don't simply focus on the monetary forms that you have to purchase. Recall that the introduction of stocks seriously depends on the general execution of the business. Right now, ought to in like manner center around the association itself. How is the association getting along in the market? Does it organize well against its adversaries? Make a point to investigate the money-related structures you hope to purchase, similarly to the association concerned.

The degree of research is, clearly, a significant task. This is one of the huge bits of trading. Also, find the components that impact a particular stock and get them. Are these segments present at the current moment? Is there any likelihood that any of these convincing factors appear later on? Given this is valid, what are the results? The more research and data you have, the better your chances of placing assets into the right monetary standards.

## Exchange with just the money you can lose

Each speculator knows about one standard: "Play with the money you can stand to lose." This is a common direction given to card sharks. Regardless of how trading fiscal structures may not be seen as wagering, especially if you don't rely upon only karma, it is so far like wagering as there is reliably the probability of losing your money. Make an effort not to use the money you prerequisite for your adolescent's enrollment or deal with nuclear family tabs. Despite the way that there is no affirmation that you will lose your money, you should simply take care of the money that you can stand to lose. Forex trading is uncommonly insecure, that it is hard to guarantee that you will make an advantage.

## Make a cut-off
This appeal is useful for fledglings. They have to pick before making any trade on a limit on to what degree will you continue grasping a losing stock, similarly for a productive one. The forex showcase is very unpredictable. Even though you can expect their incentive to increment and reduce arbitrarily, it doesn't

constantly imply a stock whose cost has quite recently diminished will before the long increment.

Some monetary forms' unpredictability is that another huge drop can at present follow a huge lessening in value. If you need your misfortunes to decrease, it is basic to limit to what degree you would grip a losing stock. Thus, you ought to acknowledge to what degree you will grip a triumphant stock. Again, whether or not a stock reliably experiences development in regard, there is so far the probability that its expense can drop definitely, about with no notification.

**Search for Chart designs**
In forex, value developments differ arbitrarily. The thing is this; abnormality makes plans. If it can't, by then, there is a more prominent opportunity to find a model. In case you can separate these models right on time, you will be one walk ahead. Remember, be that as it may, that models look like examples, and in the domain of financial guidelines, they don't prop up for particularly long.

**Watch the patterns**
Break down the diagrams and tables that show the presence of specific monetary standards. Don't simply examine their present record, yet also check their past

exhibition. This is a decent path for you to know whether the stocks are truly progressing admirably or not. Contingent upon the most recent patterns isn't fitting. Even though the most recent pattern can uncover ongoing qualities of monetary standards, you should observe that patterns regularly change. Indeed, in the forex advertise, you will scarcely observe a pattern that will keep going for a long time.

**Know the latest news**
If you are serious about trading currencies, then you should use updated news for your investing. Different factors affecting the rate of currencies are usually revealed on the news. Although the news would not state it directly, you should know that laws, businesses, economy, market behavior, and inflation, among others, can affect the prices of currencies. Observe that the news can give you significant bits of knowledge and information, but what makes a difference the most is the forex's real costs.

**Stay calm**
Terrible days do occur, and you may experience a progression of losing streaks despite benefiting some exploration. During such a minute or the minute when

you first experience your first misfortune, remain quiet. Always tell yourself this: 'stay calm.'

The forex market does not care about how you feel, so you must remain objective and focused. If you cannot control yourself, just quickly turn off your computer or mobile phone.

**Do not be greedy**
Greediness is another major problem for beginners. It is better to get small and consistent gains than lose all your money. Due to their lack of experience, many traders fall into the trap of getting the wrong forex because of keeping the stocks for too long. Do not underestimate the highly volatile nature of the forex market. Learn to trade, withdraw cash, and take full advantage of your gains.

**Don't be Emotional**
Refrain from being emotional. It is acceptable to feel enthusiastic about forex trading. But don't let your energy dazzle your judgment. Never make any exchange when under tension and treat trading forex as a business.

**Be responsible for your decisions**
Reading the assessments of "specialists" is great. However, it isn't right to let them direct your speculation choices. Shockingly, a large number of these purported

"specialists" are hacks and fakes. They advance themselves as a specialist regardless of whether their general misfortunes exceed their benefits. There are as yet a couple of genuine specialists out there; however, even the best merchants, despite everything, submit botches occasionally. The way toward building up your trading methodology is a deep-rooted venture.

Rather than depending on master guidance, you ought to build up your comprehension of the monetary market you wish to exchange and plan your procedures afterward. You should base your strategies on existing expert opinions.

**Don't chase your losses**
A trader is different from a gambler because he is the discipline in the face of loss. A trader has a set strategy that he intends to stick with. A gambler's only strategy is to get more money. A gambler, therefore, is more agitated when he is losing money than a trader. Some traders are gamblers, and this is what defines them as such. Unfortunately, the financial markets are no place for the gambler, and you will lose all your money. Chasing after your loss means breaking your strategy and investing more to recover the loss quickly. I can tell you how quickly you can blow your account this way.

Simply avoid this unfortunate happening by learning to accept your losses. If certain currencies fail to meet your expectations, learn to accept your losses by selling them and starting over again. When you seriously engage in trading forex, it is normal to lose part of your money. However, the overall idea is to maintain a winning ratio that covers these losses.

## Maintain your strategy

It is easy to get jittery either from fear or excitement and do something outside what your strategy stipulates. Try your best not to do this. There are instances where you can abandon your strategy, for example, when you can tell for sure that it will fail. Apart from these kinds of situations, maintain your strategy at all times. It helps you to measure its effectiveness and its potential.

## Only invest in currencies that have a high volume

According to some "experts," you should only invest in stocks that trade at least a hundred thousand shares per day. This serves as a safeguard against the risk of being illiquid.

## Pump your currencies

There is a motivation behind the 'pump and dump' technique. Even when there are so many individuals still monitoring such a plan: It works.

In this way, you can advertise yourself as a "specialist" in forex trading. You can set up a site and convey pamphlets to your perusers. You would then be able to buy modest monetary standards, utilize your associations to gain enthusiasm for the stocks, and sell them at a top-notch cost. If you are the sort that can persuade individuals to do what you need, at that point, this might be a simple route for you to bring in cash. Notwithstanding, if you are the sort who can't practice a touch of cunning (which is a generally excellent thing about you), at that point, you can essentially exploit individuals who siphon and dump their stocks. How? Just purchase their monetary standards, ideally before they siphon them or as ahead of schedule as could be allowed while they siphon their worth. You would then trust that their cost will expand, sell your monetary standards, and procure a few benefits.

### Keep a journal
Composing a diary can't, yet it is useful. You don't need to be an expert essayist to compose a diary. What is significant is for you to speak the truth about everything that you compose.

You can put down different things in your diary. It is additionally acceptable to compose your objectives and reasons why you need to exchange forex. Additionally, compose any exercises and mix-ups that you have learned. It is your diary, so don't hesitate to expound on everything without exception about your trading experience. A diary will permit you to consider new ideas and be a more astute merchant.

## Take a break

Forex trading has a betting component: It can be irresistible. It is something that you can accomplish for quite a long time without being worn out. It is more of leisure than work. In any case, when you participate in inquire about, which is an unquestionable requirement, that is where you will feel that trading forex includes genuine work. Permit yourself to take a break from to time. Recall that you will have better mental transparency if you allow yourself to take a rest.

## Find Updates as fast as you can

Good investors make use of up-to-date news and respond quickly. The way to take advantage of the impact of the news on stocks' prices is by taking swift trading dealings just earlier than others become conscious of them. For example, when you see that your currencies will before long experienced an enormous drop in esteem, sell them immediately. Likewise, if conceivable, know the news before it is even discharged to the general population to expand the likelihood that specific stocks will increment in esteem. The stocks ought to likewise be adequately advanced. This way, it is useful on the off chance that you can join and be dynamic in online gatherings and discussions on forex trading.

**Focus on the main pairs**
Perhaps the best thing about the forex showcase is that you can discover many new businesses. Most likely, a great number of these organizations will progress nicely. Lamentably, some of them will perform severely and even get bankrupt. However, if you figure out how to get the great new businesses' supplies early, you will wind up in a triumphant position.

You should apply the push to explore and dissect the distinctive new businesses that partake in the forex advertise along these lines. While examining a specific organization, additionally measure how it coordinates against its rivals in the market.

Developing organizations have bunches of room for upgrades, and as their benefits increase and they keep on growing, the costs of their monetary forms likewise increase.

**Have fun**

It is a common piece of advice that you should choose a job that you enjoy. In the same way, you should enjoy trading forex. If you do not enjoy it, maybe it is a signal that you should just invest elsewhere. Also, you can make better decisions when you are having fun.

**Choose the right currencies**

Always choose the right currencies to invest in. How do you know the right ones? Sufficient research. Never commence a trade without sufficient research. Take note that a little research is not enough. Researches made without serious efforts are only as good as a mere toss of a coin. Also, the most profitable and attractive-looking stocks may not always be the right currencies to invest in. After all, no matter what the media says, the forex market numbers are what counts.

**Be patient**

Patience is important when you trade currencies. Do not hurry to make a buy order simply because you have funds in your account. Also, many times, to take advantage of the high volatility of forex trading, you will have to wait for some time. Keep in mind that each activity that you make is basic. The stocks that you purchase today are the stocks that you will before long sell. Show restraint, sit tight for the best possible planning, and act in a like manner.

## Use the high volatility to your advantage

Even though numerous individuals avoid forex trading because of its high unpredictability, forex's unstable nature makes them a productive venture. With high instability, acing the well-known rule for bringing in cash is the way to benefit: purchase when the cost is low, and sell when the cost is high.

## A Few Important Notes

As a newbie, you might be somewhat stressed over beginning with forex trading. These are going to take an alternate course compared to working with conventional financial exchange alternatives. Occasionally, it is elusive that you need about the organization before making the venture you need. It is conceivable to be fruitful when utilizing monetary forms; you simply should take careful steps when in monetary standards and take as much time as is needed to get results truly. Here is some valuable advice you can begin with monetary standards to assist you with being effective include:

## Ignore some of the success stories

When you first get started with currencies, you will get a lot of information and emails about others' success stories who have done well with currencies. These are found in social media sites and emails; however, these are surprisingly surprising, or the information is completely fake.

Rather than concentrate on this, you have to take a gander at the stocks all alone and check whether they will work for you. Simply overlook the entirety of the examples of overcoming adversity since the greater part of these will be to get you to make a specific buy.

## Read through the disclaimers

If you are receiving a newsletter about currencies, you need to be careful about your reading tips. There is nothing wrong with picking out some of the stocks from these options, but you should quickly 'realize' that most of them are sales tips and to give exposure to companies that, for the most part, are bad and could end up making you lose a lot of money.

Most of the newsletters that you are going to pick tell the complete story. Many of them just want to grab and hold your attention. Important details about the right time to sell are not provided in the newsletter. The purpose of the newsletters is to get your stocks to buy their stocks by brandishing juicy figures. Always check to see whether what you are reading has a disclaimer stating that it is a promotion for a company or not. If it is, then you are reading a sales pitch. Do not expect a bit of good advice from it.

**Sell quickly**

One of the appeals that you find about forex is that you can get a tremendous ROI, up to 30 percent, in only a short measure of time. If you need to arrive at speculations like this with monetary forms, you should sell your stocks rapidly after you buy them. Tragically, rather than being content with the 30 percent or somewhere in the vicinity, individuals will get insatiable and hope to make a big comeback.

Considering currencies are sometimes getting pumped out, and the industry is volatile, you should be happy with what you get or lose out on a lot of money.

## Be careful when listening to the fund management

You should be wary about the people you are listening to the inside of currencies trading, even when it comes to funding management of the stock currencies you are working with. These companies are trying to work to get the stocks up. When the stock's up, these organizations can collect more cash, and it is more probable they will remain in business. In certain occurrences, they may not be organizations, yet fundamentally, insiders attempting to get rich.

Indeed, most of the advancements you will see originate from a similar gathering of individuals who will utilize various organizations and official statements to get some promotion and bring in some additional cash. They may have bought the stocks at a lower cost and now need to make a great deal of buzz to get you to make a buy a lot higher than what they paid.

In between the people who are using the pump and dump to make money and the companies worried about going under and want to get you to agree with them to save them from failing, it is hard to know which currencies are safe. You need to think independently of the news and some of the promotions you hear before picking out the stocks you want to invest in. With some good research and being critical of things you hear, it is easier to pick out the good currencies and make the money you want.

## Concentrate on high volume

If you are just starting, it is best just to utilize stocks that have at least one hundred thousand offers are exchanged every day. If you go with an excessively low stock in volume, it is now and then too difficult to even think about getting yourself out of this issue.

Besides, experts recommend that you pick out the stocks selling for over 50 cents a share. Going with stocks that are priced low may seem like a sensible approach, but often these aren't considered liquid enough to play with. But if you pick out stocks that are getting more than 100,000 shares a day traded and are over 50 cents for each share, you will have more luck getting them to sell nicely.

## Select the best trades from the mediocre ones

You should make sure that you pick out only the best available stocks on the market, especially when you begin in this industry. Some experts advise that traders lookout for stocks with good earnings or those that have broken through their average 52-week highs in volume. A very easy way to find these stocks is to look for stocks experiencing highs influenced by real-world economic factors and not by bogus news or hypes created to inflate their prices.

# Tips for Success

*Know when to go off-book:* While sticking to your plan, even when your emotions tell you to ignore it, is the mark of a successful trader, this in no way means that you must blindly follow your plan 100 percent of the time. You will, without a doubt, find yourself in a situation from time to time where your plan is going to be rendered completely useless by something outside of your control. You need to be aware enough of your plan's weaknesses and changing market conditions to know when following your predetermined course of action will lead to failure instead of success. Knowing when the situation is changing versus when your emotions are trying to hold sway will come with practice, but even being aware of the disparity is a huge step in the right direction.

*Avoid trades that are out of the money:* While there are a few strategies out there that make it a point of picking up options that are currently out of the money, you can rest assured that they are most certainly the exception, not the rule. Remember, the options market is not like the traditional stock market, which means that even if you are trading options based on underlying stocks buying low and selling high is not a viable strategy.

Suppose a call has dropped out of the money. In that case, there is generally less than a 10 percent chance that it will return to acceptable levels before it expires, which means that if you purchase these types of options, what you are doing is a little better than gambling. You can find ways to gamble with odds in your favor of much higher than 10 percent.

*Avoid hanging on too tightly to your starter strategy:* Your core trading strategy should always be constantly evolving as the circumstances surrounding your trading habits change and evolve as well. What's more, outside of your primary strategy, you will want to eventually create additional plans that are more specifically tailored to various market states or specific strategies that are only useful in a narrow band of situations. Remember, the more prepared you are before starting a day's worth of trading, the greater your overall profit level is likely to be; it is as simple as that.

*Utilize the spread:* If you are not entirely risk-averse, then when it comes to taking advantage of volatile trades, the best thing to do is utilize a spread as a way of both safeguarding your existing investments and, at the same time, making a profit. To utilize a long spread, you will want to generate a call and a put, both with the same underlying asset, expiration details, and share amounts but with two very different strike prices. The call will need to have a higher strike price and mark the upper limit of your profits, and the put will have a lower strike price that will mark the lower limit of your losses. When creating a spread, you must purchase both halves simultaneously. Doing it in fits and spurts can add extraneous variables to the difficult formula to adjust for properly.

*Never proceed without knowing the mood of the market:* While using a personalized trading plan is always the right choice, having one doesn't change the fact that it is extremely important to consider the market's mood before moving forward with the day's trades. First and foremost, it is important to keep in mind that the collective will of all of the traders who are currently participating in the market is just as much a force as anything that is more concrete, including market news. Even if companies release good news to various outlets and the news is not as good as everyone anticipated it to be, related prices can still decrease.

To get a good idea of the market's current mood, you will want to know the average daily numbers common for your market and be on the lookout for them to start dropping sharply. While a day or two of major fluctuation can be completely normal, anything longer than that is a sure sign that something is up. Additionally, you will always want to be aware of the major players in your market.

*Never get started without a clear plan for entry and exit:* While finding your first set of entry/exit points can be difficult without experience to guide you, you must have them locked down before starting trading, even if the stakes are relatively low. Unless you are extremely lucky, starting without a clear idea of the playing field will do little but lose your money. If you aren't sure about what limits you should set, start with a generalized pair of points and work on fine-tuning it from there.

However, more important than setting entry and exit points is using them, even when there is still the appearance of money on the table. One of the biggest hurdles that new options traders need to get over is the idea that you need to wring every last cent out of each successful trade. The fact of the matter is that, as long as you have a profitable trading plan, then there will always be more profitable trades in the future which means that instead of worrying about a small extra profit, you should be more concerned with protecting the profit that the trade has already netted you. While you may occasionally make some extra profit ignoring this advice, odds are you will lose far more than you gain as profits peak unexpectedly and begin dropping again before you can effectively pull the trigger. If you are still having a hard time with this concept, consider this: options trading is a marathon, not a sprint; slow and steady will always win the race.

*Never double down*: When they are caught up in the heat of the moment, many new options traders will find themselves in a scenario where the best way to recoup a serious loss is to double down on the underlying stock in question at its newest, significantly lowered, price to make a profit under the assumption that things are going to turn around and then continue to do so to the point that everything is completely profitable once again. While it can be difficult to let an underlying stock that was once extremely profitable go, doubling down is rarely if ever, going to be the correct decision. If you find yourself in a spot where you don't know if the trade you are about to make is going to be a good choice, all you need to do is ask yourself if you would make the same one if you were going into the situation blind, the answer should tell you all you need to know.

If you find yourself in a moment where doubling down seems like the right choice, you are going to need to have the strength to talk yourself back down off of that investing ledge and to cut your losses as thoroughly as possible given the current situation. The sooner you cut your losses and move on from the trade that ended poorly, the sooner you can start putting energy and investments into a trade that still has the potential to make you a profit.

*Never take anything personally:* It is human nature to build stories around, and therefore form relationships with, all manner of inanimate objects, including individual stocks or currency pairs. This is why it is perfectly natural to feel a closer connection to particular trades and possibly even consider throwing out your plan when one of them takes an unexpected dive. However, thinking about and acting on are two very different things, so being aware of these tendencies is so important to avoid them at all costs.

This scenario happens just as frequently with trades moving in positive directions as it does negative, but the results will always be the same. Specifically, it can be extremely tempting to hang on to a given trade much longer than you might otherwise decide to simply because it is on a hot streak that shows no sign of stopping. In these instances, the better choice of action is to sell off half of your shares instead and then set a new target based on the updated information to ensure you are in a position to have your cake and eat it too.

*Not taking your choice of broker seriously:* With so many things to consider, it is easy to understand why many new option traders simply settle on the first broker that they find and go about their business from there. However, the fact of the matter is that the broker you choose will be a huge part of your overall trading experience, which means that the importance of choosing the right one should not be discounted if you are hoping for the best experience possible. This means that the first thing you will want to do is dig past the website's friendly exterior and get to the meat and potatoes of what it is they truly offer. Remember, creating an eye-catching website is easy; filling it will legitimate information when you have ill intent is much more difficult.

First things first, this means looking into their customer service history to ensure that they treat their customers correctly and check to see that quality of service is where it needs to be. Remember, when you make a trade, every second count means that if you need to contact your broker for help with a trade, you need to know that you will be speaking with a person who can solve your problem as quickly as possible. The best way to ensure the customer service is up to snuff is to give them a call and see how long it takes for them to get back to you. If you wait more than a single business day, take your business elsewhere as if they are this disinterested in a new client, consider what the service will be like when they already have you right where they want you.

With that out the way, the next thing you will need to consider is the fees that the broker will charge in exchange for their services. There is very little regulation regarding these fees which means it will pay to shop around. In addition to fees, it is important to consider any account minimums required and any fees to withdraw the account's funds.

*Find a Mentor:* When you are looking to go from causal trader to someone who trades successfully regularly, there is only so much you can learn by yourself before you need a truly objective eye to ensure you are proceeding appropriately. This person can either be someone you know in real life or take the form of one or more people online. The point is you need to find another person or two who you can bounce ideas off of and whose experience you can benefit from. Options trading doesn't need to be a solitary activity; take advantage of any community you can find.

*Knowledge is the key:* Without some type of information you can use to assess your trades, you are playing at the roulette table. Even poker players show up to the table with a game plan. They can adapt to the circumstances and learn to read other players. That way, they can tell the contenders from the pretenders. Options trading is no different. If you cannot use the information out there to your advantage, then what you will end up with is a series of guesses that may or may not play out. Based purely on the law of averages, you have a 50/50 chance of making money. That may not seem like bad odds, but a string of poor decisions will leave you in the poor house in no time.

So, you must become familiar with the various analytics and tools you can use to your advantage. Bear in mind that everyone is going to be looking at the same information. However, it is up to you to figure out what can, or might, happen before everyone else does. This implies learning and studying the numbers to detect patterns and see where trends are headed or where trends may reverse. The perfect antidote to that is vision and foresight. Practice building scenarios. Try to imagine what could happen if trends continue. Or, what would happen if trends reversed? What needs to happen for those trends to continue or reverse?

When you ask yourself such tough questions, your knowledge and understanding begin to expand. Your mind will suddenly be able to process greater amounts of information while you generate your contingency plans based on the multiple what-ifs. That may seem like a great deal of information to handle, but at the end of the day, any time spent in improving your trading acumen is certainly worth the effort.

## Conclusion

A real option trading professional uses a reasonable cash-the-board system on each trading chance weighed against the potential danger of non-execution. This implies a real option dealer will never put all his money into one significant out of the cash position! Practical options trading professional uses exchange investigation strategies dependent on demonstrated procedures to put the chances of execution to support them and never treat each exchange as a 50/50 wager. Real options trading professional compute the measure of options influence to be utilized on each, so his portfolio is never over-utilized. A practical options trading professional doesn't hope to become wildly successful on his next exchange. He isn't going for one tremendous grand slam yet a progression of little successes that in the end includes. A real option trading professional never enables one misfortune to clear out his portfolio since he approaches the market with deference realizing that regardless of how much investigation has been led, there is dependably an opportunity that the market will neutralize him.

The next step is to step up your dedication to options trading!

It's safe to say that if you were already trading, there are probably things that you could be doing to take your options trading to the next level. Contrastingly, if you have not yet started to trade options, it's time to get in the game! Both the beginning strategies in my first book about options trading and this book have armed you with enough information to get started. The next step is to get into it. Even if this means that you're still not quite ready to begin options trading, you can still start to do more than simply read a book. For example, maybe this means that you set up meetings with a few brokers and compare commission costs, or maybe it means that you find a way to start trading in real-time via an application of some sort. The exact degree to which you want to pursue the options trading path is up to you, as long as you take the next steps towards making serious money!

The thing that matters is in ATTITUDE. Attitude oversees choices and activities. Any individual who approaches option trading with the "make easy money" attitude will likewise before long get themselves "getting-more unfortunate speedier" necessarily because these punters planning to "become showbiz royalty" on their next exchange thoroughly rejects any similarity to a transfer the board system, completely thrown away reasonable investigation for a 50/50 "wager" and remove silly from the cash positions that either become showbiz royalty or lapse useless!

Lightning Source UK Ltd.
Milton Keynes UK
UKHW022018190421
382278UK00003B/573